End CRABS IN A BARREL Syndrome

End CRABS IN A BARREL Syndrome

It's Not a Race Issue; It's a People Issue

KATRINA T. NEWSOME

DMI PUBLISHING HOUSE
WINSTON SALEM

Copyright © 2016 – Katrina T. Newsome

All rights reserved. This book is protected by the copyright laws of the United States of America. This book may not be copied or reprinted for commercial gain or profit. The use of quotations or occasional page copying for personal or group study is permitted and encouraged. Permission will be granted upon request.

Unless otherwise identified, Scripture quotations are from the King James Version. Copyright © 1982 by Thomas Nelson, Inc. Used by permission. All rights reserved.

Cover Design: Tia W. Cooke

ISBN 978-0-692-53674-2

DMI Publishing Group
(a division of Dominion Media International, LLC)
Winston-Salem, NC

Printed in the United States of America.

Dedication

This book is dedicated to my husband Rahmir Newsome and children, Demarcus, Xzavier, and Gabriel. I love you all very much and thank you for believing in me and consistently reminding me that the sky is the limit. I love you.

Acknowledgements

To my father, Eugene Thompson Sr., my mother Martha D. Thompson, and my brother Eugene Thompson Jr. – thank you all for encouraging me and being an awesome support system. I could not ask for a better group of people to call family.

To my family and friends who supported the End Crabs in a Barrel brand when it was first introduced in September 2014, THANK YOU SO MUCH FOR YOUR SUPPORT!

Contents

Introduction		11
Chapter 1:	What is Crabs in a Barrel Syndrome?	13
Chapter 2:	Who Are the Crabs In The Barrel?	19
Chapter 3:	Am I Considered A Crab In The Barrel?	25
Chapter 4:	How Can We End Crabs In A Barrel Syndrome	29
Chapter 5:	What Are The Possibilities Of Overcoming This Mentality?	33
Things to Remember		38
Conclusion		39

Introduction

The purpose of this book is to inform and make those that are not aware of what I believe is a growing epidemic in our communities. My goal is to ensure that this book is easy to read and understand. More importantly, it is necessary that it is short and concise to retain the attention of the reader. The message contained inside these pages is important because it can really transform someone's life. It is my desire that this book be used to mend broken families and other relationships.

"If you don't like something, change it. If you can't change it, change your attitude."
- *Dr. Maya Angelou*

Chapter 1

What Is "Crabs In A Barrel Syndrome?"

The term crabs in a barrel was mentioned by Marcus Garvey when he stated, "We were like crabs in a barrel, that none would allow the other to climb over, but on any such attempt all would continue to pull back into the barrel the one crab that would make the effort to climb out." In this statement, it appears that he was speaking to the African American community or maybe he was speaking to all people. Either way, the issue still exists today amongst all races in essentially everything that we do. Unfortunately, this mentality has been passed on from generation to generation and it is preventing many from reaching higher levels in life.

Crabs in a barrel mentality or syndrome is described as a group of people in like situations or environments that refuse to help each other move to a better place – hence out of the barrel – and they will do whatever they can to hold on to that individual so that they cannot rise up out of the situation. This dreadful mentality is based on individuals who consistently do nothing but intentionally insult, disrespect, gossip, and are deliberately unsupportive of those who seek a better lifestyle. They will attempt to hold back anyone who attempts to excel to a higher level. The main goal of those with this mentality is to tear down individuals trying to get out. People with this mentality may have a host of reasons for their behavior. One reason is that they are unhappy with where they are in life or what they may or may not have accomplished. Another such reason is that they may just be downright jealous because they want what someone else has attained. Their purpose is to make sure that no one gets out of the barrel including themselves because this may be comfortable or normal to someone with this horrible mentality. In fact, they may just be afraid of change. The end result of this behavior is the demise of all, if not corrected. Unfortunately, individuals with this horrible mentality do not understand that they too have the ability to improve their quality of life, but they have to get past the stinking thinking first. Take the time to unite with others versus stirring up division amongst one another; however, make sure you are uniting with a positive group of people and not a companion of fools.

A companion of fools will tear people down just because of their appearance. They may also tear others down because of the homes others live in, the cars they drive, the clothing they wear, or even their chosen line of business. They secretly hate others' differences and constantly make comparisons. Do not allow the "green eyed" monster to continue to clutch you! The saddest thing about tearing others down because of the way they look is that people have no control over this! So think about it for a moment. Why are you jealous because someone looks differently than you? It makes no sense because we were all beautifully created. Make the effort to rid yourself of insecurities or whatever it is that is causing the insecurity and stop comparing yourself to others. Focus on your own beautiful features and live your life.

Of course, many will say, "I don't do that," but what about the time that your neighbor moved to a better neighborhood and you told them not to forget where they came from. You knew deep down inside it was not about them not forgetting where they came from as much as it was you telling them, "Don't think that you are better than me." Stop secretly hating the success of others. Someone else's success should not bring pain to you. This is especially true since you have new opportunities available to you as well.

Every day we are faced with competition, some of which is friendly and some which is not. A person has to decipher who is willing to help them out of the barrel and who is not. It does not make any sense to continue trying to gain support from the same group of people who were not interested in helping or supporting you from the beginning. It is similar to the idiom of beating a dead horse. It is a futile attempt to garner support from those who refuse to applaud, celebrate, or encourage your or anyone else's success. The person who is attempting to move on to better living has to be careful because listening to someone with this mentality may discourage them from moving forward. The key is to seek those who desire to help you get out of the barrel and stick with them. Also, begin to surround yourself with people who have moved on to bigger and better things and remain loyal to them. Those who are supporting you are pushing you towards the people that can assist you. The entrepreneurs that have established a successful business can support you by introducing you to the right people so that you can also achieve your dream.

A crab in a barrel mentality is not just about a group of crabs in a barrel that refuse to get out or cannot get out. No, it is more to the story than just that thought. There has to be some sort of hidden issue within a person's being for them to not be happy for someone who succeeds and acquires better living. Someone who displays anger toward a complete stranger – or anyone for that matter – just because they are trying to improve themselves shows that they have some unresolved issues that need to be addressed. Once the issue is addressed, be honest with yourself and determine why you are jealous and envious of other people. Determine what is the root of the issue. Once the root has been discovered, you can then begin to deal with it, and only after dealing with it will you begin to see progress.

Since starting the process of really analyzing the *Crabs in a Barrel Mentality*, I've heard some say, "I'm tired of people using the metaphor of crabs in a barrel since a barrel is not the crab's natural habitat." I am going to apologize to you all from the beginning because this book is not about who put them there, but how to get them out. For example, if I was thrown in a well, I would be more concerned with how to get out instead of worrying about who threw me in the well. I would be concerned about who put me there after I got out. My purpose is to see that people recognize that they have this mentality and make a change for the better by renewing their mind. In other words, stop allowing your brain to be used to store garbage about other folks and instead use it to promote a positive way of thinking. Help someone or yourself move to a higher level without tearing down others to get there. Do not become angry because this is how Marcus Garvey labeled what he witnessed and believed to be true at the time. Be proactive and if you are not in the rut help someone else get out of the rut and then eventually we will see this mentality vanish completely. I believe that this mentality will end and I hope you do too.

Reflection
One thing that I can do today to put an end to this mentality:
1. Encourage someone
2. Speak positively about someone.
3. Put on love – genuinely encourage another's successes.

Chapter 2

Who Are The Crabs In The Barrel?

This mentality impacts homes, families, schools, workplaces, and churches. Anyone who feels they cannot help another human being because they will achieve more than them is considered a crab. You may not be able to help everybody, but you can help somebody. The home, family, school, workplace, or church is representative of the barrel. Anytime there is one person who tries to move to a better neighborhood or obtain a better job, others should encourage them to keep going and take the next step. It is unfortunate that some people will try whatever they can to discourage others from moving to a higher level. Is it right? No! What God has for you is for you and no person can take that from you. Everyone has a gift and it is up to each individual to determine what it is. The crab that gets out has discovered their own gift because God tells us in Romans 12:6 that we all have different gifts, so do not become upset when others begin to prosper in their own gift. Wait on God to reveal your gift to you.

"Jealousy only eats up your beauty. Have more faith in yourself; you got something that other people don't."
-Dr. Maya Angelou

Sometimes it appears that crabs ride each other's backs in order to get to the top. Then it appears that if they fall off of the other's back, that crab begins to hold on to the legs of the crab still thriving to get out; thus pulling them back into the barrel. Beware of those family members or friends that try to get a free ride off of your success. I am not referring to your support system; I am referring to those that have their hands stuck out as if you owe them something. Keep this in mind: the moment they can no longer ride on your back, they will then try to hold you back. Once some people realize you are no longer allowing them to consume the fruits of your labor then they may begin to speak ill of you or attempt to recruit others to stop supporting you. Be mindful of who is in your circle and why they are there or you may find yourself back in the barrel again. Continuing to communicate with people who never have anything positive to say about anyone or anything may cause you to revert back to this mentality.

Do not attempt to appease someone who will not help you or themselves. The best thing that people can do for themselves and others is to be happy for one another. We should be able to celebrate one another's successes, not waiting until a person's death to celebrate their life. Celebrating others' successes can be a stress reliever and there may be a blessing in it for you because when you do good for the sake of others God tells us that He will reward openly (see Matthew 6:4). Although helping others can be a rewarding experience, do not make it a habit of boasting about helping others for your own personal gain or only doing it because you are expecting a reward, but do it out of the sincere goodness of your heart. That one person or crab that got out of the barrel may be able to help you. The person who got out may become the next business owner or someone in a place you are seeking to go. By you supporting them, who knows how they will in return help you. Of course, if you decide to bash them or tear them down by not supporting or speaking ill about them, what do you think will happen? Sometimes we can block our own blessings by using our tongues as swords against others. The Bible declares that, *"death and life are in the power of the tongue: and they that love it shall eat the fruit thereof"* (Proverbs 18:21). Also, remember this verse: *"A soft answer turneth away wrath: but grievous words stir up anger"* (Proverbs 15:1).

I can remember speaking at a few events here and there along the way. If my family did not attend the times I spoke, I would come back and share the experience with them. Each time it appeared as if one person had a look of disinterest on their face. My dad and I were talking one day and he explained it to me this way: "A mule looks the same all the time, but a hyena laughs all of the time. Just because the mule didn't laugh does not mean that it is not with you, and just because the hyena laughs all of the time, does not mean that it was always with you." The point is do not be fooled by what people look like on the outside. At face value it may appear that they are helping you, but the moment you turn your back they may be the one tugging at your legs trying to pull you down. You cannot judge who is a crab by appearance only or by body language when you tell them your dream or goals. One thing that I have learned is if they are not for you then eventually that will show because a person cannot pretend to be something they are not forever. Eventually, the color fades and the truth will reveal itself. If there is someone who is jealous of you or just despises the fact that you obtained the very thing they desired, they will not be able to hide that emotion for long. Something will happen and force that bitterness to begin to seep out.

Remember this point as well: you cannot tell everyone your dream. One thing that I do know is what God has for you is for you. However, you cannot tell everyone your dream because if you tell it to those with a crab in a barrel mentality, they may try to discourage you from moving forward. By doing this you may not be clearly listening to God's directions for your life and you may begin to turn back to this sad mentality. Disclosing your hopes and dreams to others gives them an opportunity to shoot the thought down before you take any action. Although we may not want to admit it, we do value the opinions of others. This is why we have to be careful about who we allow in our circle of friends.

"The worst part of success is trying to find someone who is happy for you."
- *Bette Midler*

People may not believe this, but even in close relationships there may be a spouse who is envious of the other spouse. I was watching a television show recently and the husband did not want the wife to accept another position because she would be making a larger salary than he was making at his employer. He tried to discourage her by treating her crudely and refusing to talk to her. He can be considered a crab because he tried to intimidate her into not accepting the job offer, which would benefit not only her but him as well. I believe there is an evil force behind this type of behavior and it must be killed at the root. To be envious and jealous of your own spouse is definitely an issue that must be resolved or it could eventually be the cause of the dissolution of the marriage.

"Jealousy in romance is like salt in food. A little can enhance the savor, but too much can spoil the pleasure and, under certain circumstances, can be life-threatening."
- *Dr. Maya Angelou*

Reflection:
Identify people in your life who display the crab mentality and then HELP them. Be honest, it may be YOU.

1. _____
2. _____
3. _____

Chapter 3

Am I Considered A Crab In The Barrel?

Initially, a person may believe that they are anything but someone who has a crab in the barrel mentality. They will possibly believe that they are justified in being jealous of another person. Some may feel that another has taken something from them. Also, some may feel that they are not speaking critically but simply telling another how they feel about them or murmurings they heard about them. But I admonish you to beware of the person on your job who constantly talks to you unfavorably about everyone they encounter on the job, especially when the issues are those that should not be discussed with anyone other than Human Resources. This is the type of person that I would stay far away from because they are toxic and are creating a toxic environment. Apparently, they are jealous of people and in their mind they are a threat to them. Also, if they are talking to you about others, they are probably talking *about* YOU to others as well.

You have to be careful of the company you keep because hanging around a toxic person or involving yourself in toxic relationships may eventually rub off on you. It is imperative that you exit toxic relationships and do not entertain people who consistently desire to tear down others for no reason. In fact, there is never any reason to tear someone down. If you have issues with someone it is best to address it in a healthy manner. Please understand that if you are in a room where someone is bashing another and you do not step up or do anything to interfere, you are just as guilty as the one attacking. So when you are in an environment with people who insist on tearing down others, voice your concerns about the conversations and if they continue, make a conscious decision to remove yourself from that type of environment. If you refuse to speak out about the bashing sessions, some people may believe that you are in agreement with it and that it is okay to exhibit this behavior. The scripture Ezekiel 3:18 tells us *"When I say unto the wicked, Thou shalt surely die; and thou givest him not warning, nor speakest to warn the wicked from his way, to save his life; the same wicked man shall die in his iniquity; but his blood will I require at thine hand."*

"Never forget that intelligence rules the world and ignorance carries the burden. Therefore, remove yourself as far as possible from ignorance and seek as far as possible to be intelligent."
- Marcus Garvey

So the question is, "Am I considered a Crab?" This is the answer: are you the type of person who becomes jealous or envious and then begins to speak ill about someone when they receive a promotion or builds a ladder to get out of the barrel? If you will be honest and can nod your head in agreement, then YES, you may suffer from this mentality. However, there is hope! You do not have to remain a crab!

Chapter 4

How Can We End Crabs In A Barrel Syndrome?

The first step in overcoming this mentality is to recognize God as the center of your being. Once you accept Jesus Christ as your Lord and Savior, you will desire to learn more about Him. You will desire to be more Christ like, which means that you may still have struggles and challenges, but you will be able to conquer them by renewing your mind. People who already have a relationship with Christ may still battle with this mentality, but they also know that if they give this struggle to God and put it in His hands, He really does make all things new. That includes giving you a new outlook on your life where you will not compare it to others or condemn them for wanting more.

The next step is to discover what are your interests. Look in the mirror and take a hard assessment of your own life. You may find that you want to further your education, choose or change careers, or even relocate to a new state for better opportunity. It could even be something as simple as picking up a new hobby instead of sticking to the norm. Once you decide what changes are necessary to make you happy and you begin to move toward them, you will not have time to sit back and criticize others because you will be too busy improving yourself.

Finally, you must help others and yourself step out of the situation or environment that you are currently in and move to a better place. A couple of good ways to begin the process is to eliminate negative thinking and stop placing limits on yourself and what you can accomplish. Allow yourself to experiment with new ideas that promote positive growth. Moving to a better place does not mean that you literally have to pack up your belongings and move around the world (although that may be an option for you), but it does mean that you begin to visualize advancing from where you are now. We do not want to make it sound like these are simple things to do. Changing your mindset, wanting better, and doing better does not happen overnight, but if you follow these steps, you will slowly but surely transform and not only want better for yourself but want the same for others and begin to celebrate their successes as well.

Additionally, do not be afraid to see what is on the other side of where you are now. How many times have you heard that the grave is the richest place in the world because so many die with amazing ideas and gifts still bottled up inside? Just think of how much better the world would be if you began to act on your ideas. Not only would you benefit but many others as well. But how many times have people been afraid of standing out from the crowd? By doing so, they refuse to use the gift that God gave them. It is like the Bible parable of the talents where the man who was only given one talent buried it in the ground instead of cultivating and growing it. There is no time to "play it safe" or not be a good steward over the gifts God has given you. And if you are not sure of what your particular gifts and talents may be, ask God. He is more than willing to guide, direct, and provide wisdom.

Moreover, do not be afraid of what people may say or afraid of losing friends. Quite frankly, if a friend becomes upset or begins to ignore you because you desire to go after your dream, I would surmise that they really are not your friend. If this happens, it is time to find new friends and change your circle. Understand, that it does not necessarily mean that those were bad people, it just means that you have graduated from that circle and now you are on your way to your next level. You may be able to have small talk with that person, but do not get in the habit of talking to them about where you are headed because they will not understand. Unfortunately, there are some people who cannot see any further than where they have been and where they are now. Having a dream or goal that is beyond the dreams of others around you may cause discomfort. You may be surprised at who appears closer than a brother to you right now, but when it is time to build the foundation of where you are going, they are nowhere to be found. They may even be found standing on the side line throwing stones at your glass house. However, do not get discouraged by this sudden shift in your life; instead grow excited because you are on your way to the next level with new people and new opportunities and possibilities. You will never know what you can become or what you should become without going the extra mile and leaving the naysayers behind.

End the crabs in a barrel mentality by encouraging one another to go the extra mile. Help support and promote others' goals whenever possible even though you may not see or understand their vision the way they see it. I can assure you that the support that you give to another person will not only make them feel good, but it will also put a smile on your face as well. Real support is not openly applauding others and secretly despising or envying them behind their backs. Be sincere about your support. You never know just how much that means to another when they see they are not alone, and you are cheering them on toward the finish line.

Chapter 5

What Are The Possibilities Of Overcoming This Mentality?

Today, let's stop labeling this mentality a race problem. It is not a race or color issue; it is a people issue and can be found among every race, ethnicity, and socioeconomic status. However, the possibilities of building a new future for ourselves and the generations to come are endless. The sky is truly the limit. New businesses will be opened and prosper if we stick together and give our support to them at the beginning and continually. But, if we do not begin to get rid of this mentality, things will not change for the better. In fact, the negative will be amplified. Pursue your own dreams and adventures so you will know what that experience feels like, and you may find that you not only enjoy getting out of the barrel but find satisfaction in pulling someone else out as well. You can be the one that escapes from the barrel and decides to help others. Someone once told me that if you put one crab in a barrel then it is sure to get out, but the moment you put two or three in there they will attempt to pull each other down.

Let's look at this a little deeper. Imagine a place where at least one or two positive people in a room decide to inspire someone else. They make the decision to help someone instead of pulling them down. Can you imagine the number of presidents, CEO's or new business owners that will be born? There could be tremendous growth within every neighborhood if just one person purposed to stop being negative about everything and everyone.

You may not even realize how much stress this miserable mentality causes, but when you try to compare yourself to other people it can be a real burden when in your mind you are still coming up short. That way of thinking can be stressful and too much stress can lead to physical illness and disease. However, negative thinking does not have a place in your thoughts when the only person that you are competing with is yourself and becoming a better you.

Think about this for a moment. If on your job someone receives a promotion and you become upset about it, what is the effect? One would have to be drawn to the conclusion that it has a negative impact. Could it be that you did not work as hard as the one promoted or are you upsetting yourself over a promotion that may not have been intended for you? Remember, that promotion comes from God and He makes no mistakes about who He gives them to. It could be as simple as changing your attitude and being supportive of your colleague, and the next promotion could be yours for the taking. For your own sake quit harboring the negative feelings.

This brings me to my next point. Are we demonstrating this mentality in front of our own children? Today children have more than enough issues they have to face in their everyday lives and they definitely can do without this mentality being displayed in front of them. Children are like sponges and they absorb the behavior they see and imitate it. If there is a parent in the home that consistently tears everyone down, then the children are likely to do the same thing. Fortunately, this type of behavior can be eliminated before it contaminates the entire home. Instead of tearing down other relatives, the neighbors, or anyone else with your words, celebrate their successes. If this is challenging for you, then it may be best to resort to silence, but please don't exhibit the crab mentality in front of your children and pass on the habit to them.

I can remember when I was growing up my mom used to say, "I never try to keep up with anyone," whenever she saw someone who was obviously in a competition of their own. This is what this whole mentality is about – if I cannot get it, then neither can nor should you. What a sad way to live your life.

Instead, consider working toward your goals or dreams and not giving up. There is one thing that I have learned and that is what is for me is for me. There is not one single soul that can take it away. We have to remember that sometimes when things are taken out of our grasp it is for our best interest. Of course, at first it appears like our world may end at any moment, but we have to look pass things and people that we have lost along the way. These things or folks were never meant to go with us to our destiny anyway. This is a message we should begin teaching our children at a young age – do not try to hold back your peers but help each other and watch the wonderful possibilities unfold. Once this message is embedded in our minds, the accomplishments are limitless.

Carefully consider reading this book to your children at a young age and help them understand what it means to help someone else. They understand more than we think they know. Pull out that ugly sucker branch, meaning this mentality, before it takes root in their lives. Unfortunately, if we do not speak to our children about this issue and educate them early on, someone else will and it may not be the positive message that needs to come forth.

We also have to remember we live in a world where the opportunities are endless. The only reason someone may feel threatened or feel incapable of achieving success is because they are trapped in their own mind. You have created a prison in your own mind which holds only one prisoner and that's YOU! Regardless of your past you can achieve the dream God has for you. He may not desire you to be the greatest singer in the world, but he may have chosen you to be the greatest singer in your community. Do not base your success on what people have to say, many who have not even discovered their own purpose. The Bible states, *"Do not pay attention to every word people say, or you may hear your servant cursing you"* (Ecclesiastes 7:21).

We have not begun to touch the surface of this issue but rest assured that we are definitely headed towards correcting the problem.

Things to Remember in Our Actions and When Speaking

1. Promote positivity.

2. Before you speak, THINK!

3. Does what you say help others or tear others down?

4. Be honest.

5. Does it have anything to do with you?

6. Does what you have to say line up with the Word of God?

7. Are you being hurtful or helpful?

8. Are you speaking out of envy and jealousy or love?

9. Do your words stir up trouble or strife?

10. Will God be pleased with what you are saying?

Conclusion

You are the only person who can control your actions and thoughts. Therefore do yourself and others a favor by losing the bad attitude towards others just because you are jealous or envious of someone or something. You have no idea what that person had to endure to get to where they are or have the things they have. Some of us would be baffled to learn what our co-workers, church family, or anyone else, has to endure in their daily lives. Stop belittling others just because gossiping about them makes you feel better about yourself. Please, by all means, change your mindset. We have all heard the saying, "Change Your Mindset, Change Your Life." Well I believe this to be true and I have found that once I make up my mind I can achieve anything. I encourage each and every one of you to change your mindset today and promote positivity for the rest of your life!

"HATE…..It has caused a lot of problems in this world, but it has not solved one yet."
- *Dr. Maya Angelou*

About the Author

Katrina Newsome, a native of Brunswick County, VA is a graduate of Liberty University. She holds a certificate in Professional Life Coaching, and has helped innumerable people during the past decade with personal and professional empowerment, providing support and clarity in making life work. Katrina established End Crabs in a Barrel LLC in 2014 which is an organization with the goal of empowering others to unite and not divide, and being helpers of one another. She is the wife of SFC Rahmir Newsome and mother to three sons, Demarcus, Xzavier, and Gabriel. Her literary debut, "End Crabs in the Barrel Syndrome" is sure to resonate with many and tear down this mentality that has held many captive for far too long.

To contact the author for speaking engagements, conferences, book tours and book signings, write or call:
Visit www.endcrabsinabarrel.com
E-mail: endcrabsinabarrel@gmail.com
Phone: (804) 410-5902

Other Authors by
DMI PUBLISHING HOUSE

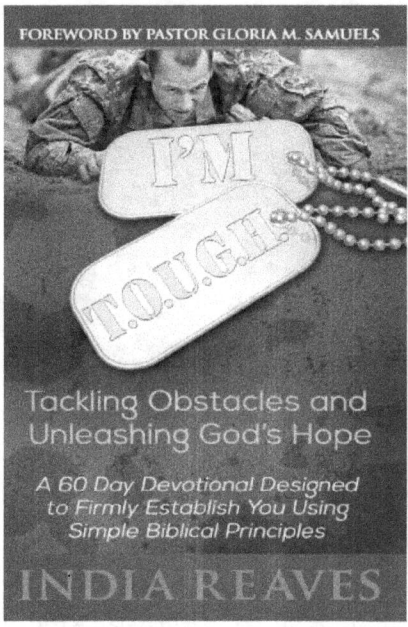

I'm T.O.U.G.H is a 60 day devotional book intended to resolutely ground the reader in a strong spiritual foundation. The messages in this book thrust the reader to think and reflect on their own lives and situations and to dig deep in themselves and be contingent on the victor that is in each and every one of us. Through scriptures, stories, personal testimonies, and teachings, readers will grasp hold to the fact that they are built to last.

ISBN: 978-0-6922-0263-0

For more information, visit
www.imtoughdevotional.com

Other Authors by
DMI PUBLISHING HOUSE

Devastated But Not Destroyed is a divine interruption for those who may be headed towards destruction. It will jolt your faith, sustain your strength, and change your perspective from one of pity and pain to that of power. Discover how to master the moments of your life, pack up the pity party for good, and embrace the challenge of change. Everyone at some point will experience devastation, and this book serves as the go-to guide to rediscover the tenacity and fortitude necessary to avoid the pitfalls of destruction.

ISBN: 978-0-692-34201-5

For more information, visit
www.devastatedbutnotdestroyed.com

Other Authors by
DMI PUBLISHING HOUSE

We speak of spiritual warfare in the same mindset as physical warfare. We have approached it with thoughts of violent and vehement confrontations. In actuality, spiritual warfare is best fought using simple biblical principles. 100 out of 100 people are offended, the offender, or both. This book is intended to teach one of the most basic, yet most powerful principles - and that is the principle of forgiveness. As you begin to practice this principle, you will experience a freedom in your spirit that you have longed to have.
ISBN: 978-0-692-30523-2

For more information, e-mail
scvinson@gmail.com

www.ingramcontent.com/pod-product-compliance
Lightning Source LLC
Chambersburg PA
CBHW072115290426
44110CB00014B/1925